FAVOURITE Bible Stories

Creation stories
Since time began many cultures have invented stories that explain the origin and order of the universe. One of the most famous is the Babylonian epic of creation, "Enuma Elish". The Babylonian version features the god Marduk. A later Assyrian version substitutes the national god Asshur for Babylon's Marduk. The story opens in the time before the earth and order have been brought into being.

Fruit
The law of Moses declared that for the first three years after a tree was planted, its fruit was forbidden. In the fourth year, the fruit belonged to God, and it was only after five years that people could eat the tree's fruit. Fruit trees were so valuable that even during war, special efforts were made to protect them. Figs, grapes, dates and olives are all important crops, but citrus fruits did not come in until New Testament times.

Leopard
The Bible tells us that every living creature was created by God, although it does not tell us how different species of animal changed over time. The expression that "leopards don't change their spots" has its origins in the Bible.

GOD MAKES THE WORLD

✤ Genesis 1-2 ✤

At the beginning of time, God created heaven and earth. The earth was completely dark, without any shape, and empty. Complete darkness hung over the ocean waters.

God then made everything simply by the power of speaking out his commands.

"Let the light shine!" God said on the first day, and light came. He saw that the light was good. He separated the light and the darkness. He called the light "day", and the darkness "night". Then came evening and morning.

On the second day, he said, "Let the oceans divide," and a great space appeared between the waters. God called this space "sky".

On the third day, God said, "Let there be dry ground," and he called the dry ground "land". Then the land produced many different kinds of trees and flowers. Fruit and crops started to grow.

On the fourth day, God commanded, "Let the sky be filled with lights," and he made the sun, and the moon, and set brilliant stars and galaxies around them.

On the fifth day, God filled the oceans with fish and the sky with birds. He blessed them all and told them to roam free and to increase in number and to fill the earth and skies and oceans.

Finally, on the sixth day, God made animals of all shapes and sizes, both tame and wild, to live on the land. And he made men and women, and told them, "Go and have many children so you can take care of the earth and all the fish, birds and animals and all living creatures."

At the end of the sixth day, the heavens and the earth were completed in all their glory. God looked back at everything he had made and was extremely pleased with what he saw.

By the seventh day, God had finished making the universe. So he rested from all his work and made this day a special day. It was a holy day, a day for rest and for stopping to give thanks for all the wonders of his magnificent creation.

The fifth day of creation
The opening words of the Bible declare that God made heaven and earth. Everything around us did not come about by mere chance but is the result of God's purpose and design.

ADAM AND EVE SPOIL CREATION

✤ Genesis 2-3 ✤

The tree of knowledge
According to tradition, the fruit that Adam and Eve ate from the tree of knowledge was an apple. But the Bible does not tell us what kind of tree or fruit it was. Some experts now think the fruit may even have been a pomegranate.

God made a beautiful garden called Eden, a paradise full of animals and fruit trees. At the centre of the garden stood a tree with the special power to give the knowledge of good and evil to anyone who ate its fruit. God told Adam, the first man, to look after the plants, but warned him, "You may eat fruit from any tree you like, but not from the tree of knowledge. If you do, you will die."

When God realized that Adam was lonely by himself, he made him fall into a deep sleep. He took out one of Adam's ribs and from it he made a woman called Eve, to be Adam's wife. Although they were both naked, they were not in the least embarrassed, and they were very happy living in the garden.

Now in the garden was a snake, who was the most cunning of all the animals. He used his powers of persuasion to get Eve into trouble. "You won't really die if you eat fruit from the tree of knowledge," he said. "Instead you will be just like God, knowing what is good and what is evil."

Eve was so tempted by the tasty fruit that would make her clever that she picked some and ate it. She offered some to Adam, who ate it too. Immediately, they realized that they were naked and were ashamed. They sewed fig leaves together as clothes to cover themselves.

When God came walking in the garden that evening, Adam and Eve hid themselves behind the trees in fear. "Adam, where are you?" God called. "Have you eaten the fruit I told you not to eat?"

Reluctantly, Adam had to admit that he had. "The snake tricked me into giving it to him," Eve explained, sadly.

God was angry that Adam and Eve had disobeyed him, and told Adam, "I will curse the ground with weeds, so that you will have to work hard to grow your food." Then God told Adam and Eve to leave the Garden of Eden for ever.

CAIN MURDERS ABEL

✤ Genesis 4 ✤

Adam and Eve started a new life outside the Garden of Eden. They had two sons: Abel, who grew up to be a shepherd, and Cain, who worked in the fields as a farmer.

When the time came to make an offering to God, Cain brought a few of his harvest crops, but he did so with a careless attitude. Abel, on the other hand, brought only the very best pieces of meat from his sheep, showing his deep, heartfelt trust in God. So God was pleased with Abel's offering but not with Cain's. This filled Cain with anger.

"Why are you so angry?" God asked Cain. "If you make the right offering I will accept it, but be careful, because if you do not, sin is waiting to pounce on you and rule you."

But Cain would not listen. Burning with rage and jealousy, he lured his brother Abel into a field and killed him.

"Where is your brother?" God asked him, but Cain pretended not to know.

"Don't ask me," he replied. "Am I supposed to look after him?"

"Look what you've done!" said God, angrily. "I can plainly see Abel's blood on the ground, so now I must punish you. From now on your crops will no longer grow and you will have to wander through the world without a home."

Cain trembled with fear. "My punishment is too much for me to bear," he pleaded with God. "Because you are no longer my friend, whoever finds me will kill me."

"Don't worry," God replied, showing mercy by putting a special mark on Cain to protect him. "If anyone kills you, he will suffer seven times more than you." So, with tremendous sadness, Cain left and went to live in the land of Nod.

Cain kills Abel
After Adam and Eve were expelled from the Garden of Eden, sin entered the world for the first time. This is shown when Cain became jealous of Abel and committed the first murder. Cain's punishment for killing his brother was to become a wanderer with no home. He was forced to lead a nomadic existence in the land of Nod.

The Garden of Eden
We do not know the precise location of the Garden of Eden. A popular theory is that it lay in the lush and fertile area of land between the rivers Tigris and Euphrates in Mesopotamia.

NOAH BUILDS THE GREAT ARK

✤ Genesis 6-8 ✤

Carpenters' tools
More than three thousand years ago, the Egyptians used tools like this adze and chisel. Noah would have used an adze to hack and plane the wood, and a chisel to carve and shape it.

Boat building
In many parts of the world, boats are still built by hand using methods and tools that have hardly changed over thousands of years. The ark that Noah built was enormous. It is estimated that it was about as long as two jumbo jets and higher than a five-storey building. The framework was sealed with tar to make it watertight.

God saw that people were becoming more and more wicked and he began to regret making them.

But there was one good man, called Noah, who loved and obeyed God. "I have decided to destroy the men and women that I have created," God told him. "Every living animal will die too. I want you to make a wooden boat, because I am going to send a flood to cover the whole world. Only you and your family, and the animals that are inside the boat, will be kept safe."

With the help of his three sons, Noah obeyed God and began to build an enormous boat, called an ark. He followed the plans that God had given him for its construction precisely. When the ark was finished, God sent two of every kind of animal and bird – one male and one female – and they all went into the ark. As soon as the last animals were on board, God told Noah and his family to get in, too. God himself closed the door behind them.

Then it began to rain. Water poured down from the sky and burst up from springs deep under the earth's surface. Soon the ark was floating free on the swirling waves that crashed against it. The water kept rising until even the tallest mountains were covered and the last remaining animals and people had drowned.

After several months, the rain stopped and the water began to go down. The ark drifted silently over the calm waters until finally it came to rest on the mountains of Ararat. Noah sent out birds to see how much of the earth was free of flooding. When a dove returned with a fresh olive leaf in its beak, Noah knew that the trees were growing again. Their voyage was over. Soon they could all leave the ark and explore the earth.

A RAINBOW OF PROMISES

✣ Genesis 8-9 ✣

"You must leave the ark now," God said to Noah and his family. "Bring the animals, too, as they must find new homes and raise their young." So Noah climbed down the gangway and stepped onto the earth. He was so glad that God had saved him from the flood that he built an altar and made an offering to God.

"Even though people will never change, and will continue to behave wickedly, I will not destroy the world in this way again," God said. "From now until the end of time I promise that the rhythm of nature will continue. There will be a time for sowing seeds and for reaping the harvest, and the hot summer will follow the cold winter as surely as the day follows the night."

Then God told Noah and his family, "Make a fresh start. The whole world belongs to you and your children. Use it wisely and enjoy its resources."

Then God made a covenant with Noah, his children, and all the animals. "I will never again send a flood to destroy the world. If ever it rains for a long time and you begin to worry that I have forgotten this promise, all you need to do is look upwards. I will put a sign in the sky to remind you of what I have said. Whenever you see the colourful rainbow shining out in the middle of dark rain clouds, remember my promise."

The rainbow
There are lots of covenants in the Bible, but God's covenant with Noah is the first one. A covenant is an agreement in which people promise to do certain things. The rainbow was the sign of God's covenant promise never again to destroy the earth with a flood. The word that the Bible uses for rainbow also means a "war-bow". This symbolizes God lowering his bow to declare peace.

BABBLING TONGUES

✤ Genesis 11 ✤

Mud bricks
Today in the Middle East people still make bricks in the same way as they would have done to build the tower of Babel. The wet mud or clay is shaped in a wooden mould and then pressed out to dry in the sun or baked in kilns for greater durability.

The tower of Babel
The tower of Babel may have been a type of Babylonian temple, called a ziggurat. Ziggurats were pyramid-shaped and some may have been over 100 metres high. They had steps on the outside and a temple at the top. Sometimes each level was painted a different colour so the building would have looked like a large rainbow.

Sites of ziggurat towers
From earliest times, people have known they should worship God, so they built temples. Ruins of these temples have been found all over ancient Mesopotamia, which lies in modern-day Iraq. The traditional site of the tower of Babel was Babylon, one of the chief cities founded by Nimrod.

At first, Noah's descendants roamed from place to place in the east. But many years later, one group reached a fertile plain in Babylonia and decided to settle down there.

The people held a meeting and decided to build themselves a large city to live in. They would use bricks made of mud and straw baked hard in the fiercely hot sun, and they would stick them together with tar. The grandest building was to be a spectacular tower, so tall that its top would reach to the clouds.

So the people eagerly set to work building their new city.

"Now we will have a proper home and will no longer have to keep on wandering through the world. And when people realize how clever we've been to build such a grand city, then we'll be famous," they told each other, proudly.

But their pride was to be their downfall. When God looked carefully at their growing city with its elaborate tower, he was not pleased.

"These people are vain. They have forgotten me and only think of how important they are," said God. "If I let them continue, soon they will want to control everything in the world. But I will stop them by mixing up their words so that they cannot understand each other. Then they will not be able to carry out their plans."

Soon all that could be heard across the city was a confused babble of voices. Building work had to come to a halt, because no one could understand what his neighbour was trying to say. The people all spoke different languages, and could not communicate with each other, so they went to live in different parts of the world.

GOD CALLS ABRAHAM

✣ Genesis 12-13 ✣

One of Noah's descendants was a man called Abraham, who grew up in the city of Ur in Mesopotamia. His father decided to move the family to Canaan, but on the way they settled in the city of Haran. There, Abraham and his wife Sarah enjoyed a life of wealth. They had many servants, and owned large flocks of cattle, sheep and donkeys.

One day, when Abraham was seventy-five years old, God told him something that would change his life for ever. "You and your family must leave your country and travel to the land of Canaan. There I will bless you and make you the father of a great nation."

Abraham had a deep faith that what God said would come true. So he loaded all his possessions onto his camels and set out on the long journey with Sarah, his nephew, Lot, and all their servants.

When they reached Canaan, God appeared to Abraham and made him the wonderful promise that one day Abraham's children would live there. Sarah had not been able to have any children, but being a man of faith, Abraham believed that in the future God's promise would come true.

But it was proving difficult to find enough grazing pasture for all the animals. Abraham's shepherds started to fight Lot's shepherds for each piece of grass.

Abraham settled the argument wisely. "We should split up and go our separate ways," he told Lot, and he gave Lot first choice as to where he could go.

So Lot set off with his flocks for the fertile Jordan Valley, while Abraham stayed in Canaan.

Golden bull's head
Archaeologists have found the site of Ur, the city that Abraham came from. There they have discovered royal graves containing many exquisite gold objects, such as this golden head of a bull, set with precious stones. It once formed part of a lyre – a musical instrument similar to a harp. These finds show that Ur was a powerful, wealthy and sophisticated city.

A BEAUTIFUL BRIDE FOR ISAAC

✤ Genesis 24 ✤

When Abraham was nearing the end of his life, he began to think about finding a wife for his son, Isaac. He did not want Isaac to marry a woman from Canaan, where they were living.

So Abraham sent for one of his servants. He told the servant that God would help him to find a bride for Isaac among the family's relatives in their homeland of Mesopotamia.

The servant set off, and when he arrived outside the city where Abraham's brother Nahor lived, he let his tired camels rest near a well.

He prayed, "Lord God, please may one of the young women coming to the well be the bride you have chosen for Isaac. When I ask her for water, let her offer to water my camels, too, so that I may know she is the right woman."

Even before he had finished praying, a beautiful young woman called Rebecca, who was Nahor's granddaughter, arrived to fill the water jar on her shoulder.

"Please give me a drink of water from your jar," the servant said.

"Gladly, sir," Rebecca replied, "and I will also bring water for your camels."

The servant was delighted that his prayer had been answered. Rebecca was the right one! He praised God, and gave her gifts of jewellery.

"Is there room for me to stay at your father's house?" he asked.

"You are very welcome," she replied.

Rebecca's father and brother welcomed the servant, who gave them gifts from Abraham. They listened carefully to his story about how God had chosen Rebecca to be Isaac's wife, and they happily agreed to the marriage. The next morning, Rebecca said goodbye to her family and travelled back to Canaan with the servant.

When they drew near, they saw Isaac walking in the fields. Rebecca got down from the camel to meet her new husband, shyly covering her face with her scarf.

When he heard the servant's story, Isaac was delighted to meet his beautiful bride, and took Rebecca into his tent and married her. And Isaac loved Rebecca very much.

Water jars
Pottery water jars like these have been used for centuries to fetch water from wells. Their size and shape has changed little over the years. In many dry parts of the world today, wells are still the main source of water for people and their animals.

JACOB TAKES ESAU'S BLESSING

✤ Genesis 25-27 ✤

For many years, Isaac's wife Rebecca was unable to have children. Then at last she gave birth to twin sons, Esau and Jacob. Before they were born, God told Rebecca that he planned to make Jacob the head of the family, even though he was younger than his brother Esau.

One day, Esau came home from hunting feeling very hungry, so he asked Jacob to give him a portion of the lentil stew he was cooking.

"Only if you give me your rights as the first-born son," Jacob replied.

"All right," agreed Esau, greedily taking the food without caring too much about losing his inheritance. "I am about to die of hunger anyway. What good would my rights be to me then?"

Years later, when Isaac knew he was coming to the end of his life, he wanted to put his affairs in order. "Go and kill an animal for me, Esau, and cook me a tasty meal. Then I will give you my final blessing before I die."

Rebecca was listening, and decided to make God's plan for Jacob come true. "I will cook your father a meal," she told Jacob, "then you can pretend to be Esau and receive your father's blessing instead."

Jacob protested, "Father is almost blind, but I am not hairy like Esau, so he will know that it is me."

Rebecca answered by dressing Jacob in Esau's best clothes, and putting goat-skins on his arms and neck to make him feel hairy.

"Are you really Esau?" Isaac asked, when Jacob took him the meal.

"I am," Jacob lied, hoping to trick his father.

Isaac recognized the smell of Esau's clothes and felt his hairy arms. Believing it was Esau, he gave Jacob his blessing to be in charge of the family when he died.

So when Esau arrived home shortly afterwards and brought his father his meal, Isaac was shocked to discover he'd been tricked. "Your cunning brother deceived me and stole your blessing," Isaac told him, in great distress.

Esau exploded with anger and begged his father, "You must bless me, too!" but there was nothing Isaac could do.

CHEATING

Cheating is dishonest. It's not fair if someone at school gets a better mark than us because they have cheated. We may feel angry with them and that we can't trust them any more. People who cheat never get away with it; in the end they usually get found out and punished.

Lentils and beans
Lentils and beans are a favourite food throughout the Near East. They can be boiled to make stew, like the one that Jacob gave to Esau, or they can be mixed with other ingredients to make bread.

Lentil plant
The lentil is a member of the pea family. It is a small plant, with five or six pairs of tendril-bearing leaves on each stem. It has white-and-violet striped flowers with flat pods which encase the lentils.

JOSEPH'S DREAMS

✤ Genesis 37 ✤

Jacob had twelve sons, but it was Joseph who had a special place in his heart, because he was Rachel's son. To show everyone that Joseph was his favourite, Jacob gave him a fabulous coat to wear. It had long sleeves and was made of fine material woven in all the colours of the rainbow.

All Joseph's brothers were jealous of him, and it didn't help that Joseph told Jacob every time his brothers did something wrong. In fact, his brothers hated Joseph so much that they were hardly pleasant to him at all.

One night, Joseph had an unusual dream. "In my dream," Joseph told his brothers, "we were all working in the fields, tying up bundles of wheat, when suddenly my bundle stood up straight and your bundles bowed down to it."

His brothers were not impressed. "Do you really think you are going to rule over us?" they asked, and hated him all the more.

Later, Joseph boasted to his eleven brothers about another dream, which made them even more angry. "Listen to this!" he said. "In my dream I saw the sun, the moon, and eleven stars bowing down to me!"

He told his father about the dream, but even Jacob was annoyed with him and told Joseph off. "Do you really think that your mother and I and all your brothers are going to bow down to you? Don't be so ridiculous!"

But once Jacob had calmed down, he wondered about the dream. Perhaps Joseph had been specially chosen by God to be a leader and the dream would come true, after all.

JOSEPH SOLD AS A SLAVE

✣ Genesis 37 ✣

One day, Jacob sent Joseph to check on his brothers. They were in the fields, looking after their flocks of sheep. By now, Joseph's brothers were so full of hatred and jealousy that they wanted to kill him. They were just waiting for a good opportunity to put their plan into action.

"Look, here comes the dreamer," they sneered, spotting Joseph in the distance wearing his fancy coat of many colours. "Let's kill him and throw his body into a dry well, then all his dreams will come to nothing! We can pretend that a wild animal killed him, so that we do not get into trouble."

But the eldest brother, Reuben, protested, saying, "Don't kill him. Let's just throw him into one of these wells." He secretly hoped to come back later and help Joseph to escape.

So when Joseph arrived, the brothers pulled off his fine coat and threw him into a dry well. Then they sat down to eat, ignoring Joseph's cries for help.

A little later, one of the brothers, Judah, noticed a group of Ishmaelite traders passing by on their camels, on their way to Egypt. He said to the others, "I have an idea. Why don't we sell Joseph as a slave, instead of murdering him, then we won't feel so guilty. After all, he is our brother."

His brothers agreed, so when the next group of Ishmaelite traders came past, they pulled Joseph out of the well and sold him to them for twenty pieces of silver. The brothers did not care that Joseph would face a hard life as a slave.

To cover up what they had done, they killed a goat and dipped Joseph's coat into its blood, then took it to show their father.

Jacob was horrified when he saw it. "It is Joseph's coat!" he wailed. "He has been torn to pieces by a wild animal!"

Jacob was so upset that no one could comfort him, and he mourned his favourite son for a very long time.

Dyes
Bright and colourful dyes like these can be found on sale in many Middle Eastern markets today. But the Bible only mentions four colours of dye – purple, blue, crimson and scarlet. These dyes would have been made from natural products such as shellfish, insects and plant roots.

Coat tassels
The Greek translation of the Bible describes Joseph's coat as a "coat of many colours", but it would be more accurately translated as a richly decorated, long-sleeved robe. It was probably made from cloth woven with coloured thread and fringed with tassels around the hem.

Camel traders
Traders like this Bedouin with his camels would have been a familiar sight in Joseph's day. Camels allowed traders to carry heavy goods through desert areas. The Ishmaelite traders in this story would probably have been carrying spices and incense to sell in Egypt.

THROWN INTO PRISON

✣ Genesis 39 ✣

Egyptian queen
Wall paintings discovered from ancient Egyptian tombs tell us a lot about how these people lived. Fine linen clothes and elaborate jewellery were typical dress for noblewomen like Potiphar's wife. This queen holds the ankh symbol, which represents eternal life. Only gods, kings and queens could carry this symbol as only they had the power to give or take away life.

Once they reached Egypt, the Ishmaelite traders sold Joseph as a slave. He was bought by a man called Potiphar, who had an important job as captain of the guards at the Egyptian king's palace. Potiphar soon realized that Joseph was a hard-working man, and that God was making him successful in everything he did. So he put Joseph in charge of his house and trusted him with everything he owned.

But trouble lay ahead. Because Joseph was a strong, attractive man, Potiphar's wife began to desire him and tried to persuade him to make love to her.

Joseph was horrified and told her firmly, "Your husband has trusted me with everything in this house, but he certainly has not given you to me. I will not sin against God by doing such a terrible thing!"

But Potiphar's wife would not give up. Every day, she kept trying to persuade him. But still Joseph would not give in to temptation, and he did his best to avoid being near her.

Then one day, when none of the other servants were around, Potiphar's wife grabbed Joseph by his coat and insisted that he go to bed with her. Luckily, Joseph managed to escape from her, but as he ran off he left his coat behind in her hands.

"Look what Joseph has done!" Potiphar's wife cried out to her servants, pretending to be very upset. "He tried to force me into bed, but I screamed and he ran off!"

When her husband, Potiphar, came home, she showed him Joseph's coat and told him the same terrible lies, and he believed her. Angrily, he ordered Joseph's arrest and had him thrown into prison.

Calamity had struck Joseph, but God was with him, even in prison. The prison guard soon realized that Joseph could be trusted, and helped him by putting him in charge of all the other prisoners. Everything in the prison ran smoothly, because God helped Joseph succeed in everything that he did.

Eye make-up
Egyptian women wore a lot of make-up. Different minerals, like galena or lead ore – which makes kohl, for example – were ground down and then mixed with water to make a paste. The paint was kept in a tube and applied with a little stick of wood or bronze. Archaeological discoveries from Egypt have unearthed many examples of tubes and pots like this one made from painted pottery.

TELL ME WHAT MY DREAMS MEAN

✤ Genesis 40-41 ✤

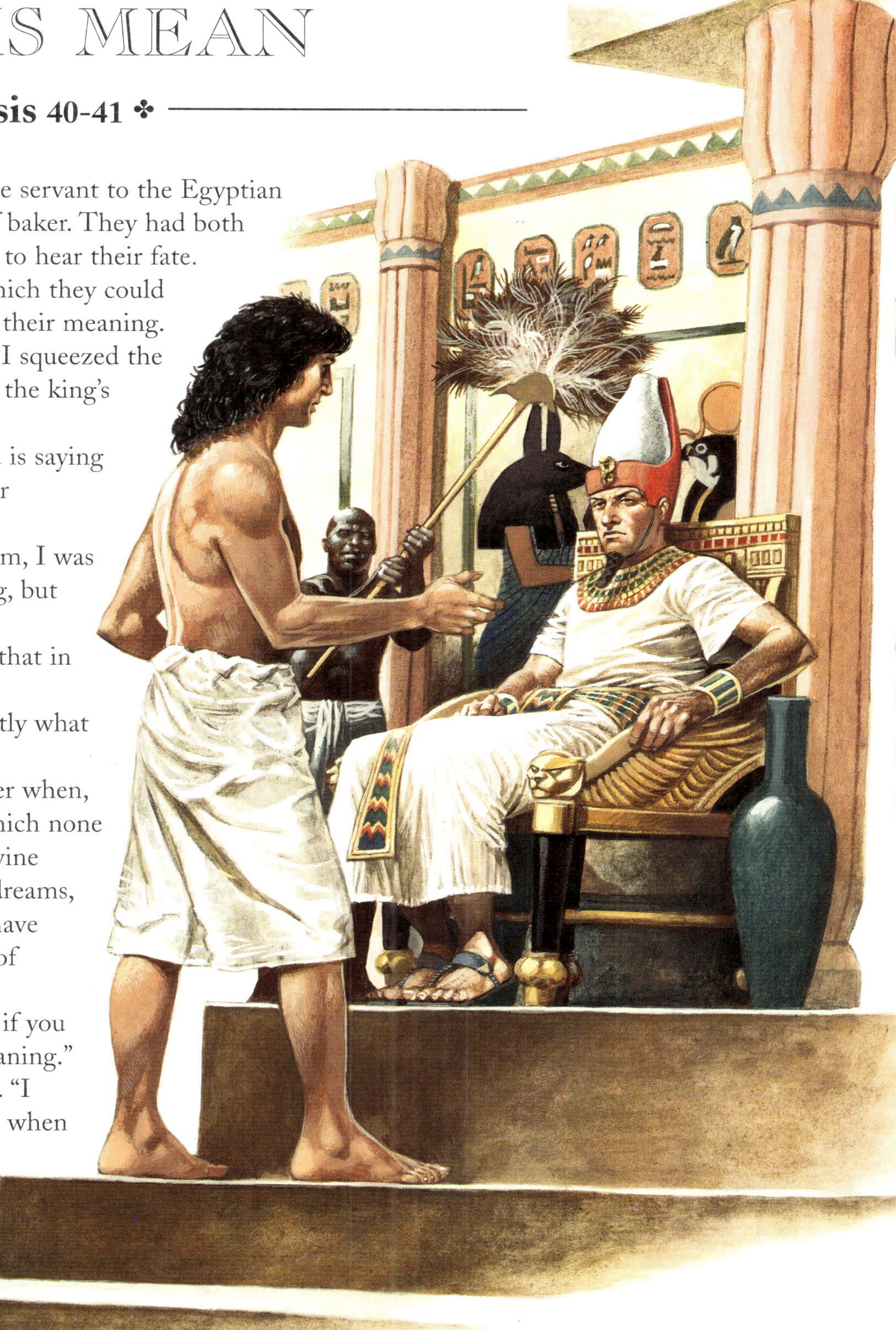

While he was in prison, Joseph became servant to the Egyptian king's wine steward and to his chief baker. They had both angered the king and were in prison waiting to hear their fate. One night, both men had strange dreams which they could not understand, so Joseph offered to explain their meaning.

The wine steward said, "In my dream, I squeezed the juice from the grapes on three branches into the king's wine cup."

Joseph was delighted to tell him, "God is saying that in three days, the king will give you your job back."

Then the chief baker said, "In my dream, I was carrying three baskets of pastries for the king, but the birds were eating them up."

Joseph told him, sadly, "God is saying that in three days, the king will cut off your head."

And three days later, the king did exactly what Joseph had told them.

Joseph was still in prison two years later when, one night, the king had a puzzling dream which none of his wise men could interpret. When the wine steward told him that Joseph could explain dreams, the king summoned Joseph from prison. "I have been told that you can explain the meaning of dreams," he said.

Joseph carefully replied, "I cannot, but if you give me the details, God will tell me the meaning."

So the king began to relate his dreams. "I dreamt that I was standing by the river Nile, when seven fat cows came out of the river to eat grass. Then seven thin cows appeared and ate the fat cows. I also dreamt that I saw seven ripe ears of corn, which were swallowed by seven thin, scorched ears of corn. Tell me, what does it all mean, Joseph?"

"God is telling you to prepare yourself for seven years of plentiful harvests, followed by seven years of terrible famine," Joseph explained. "You must put a clever man in charge of the country at once. Only if you save food wisely while it is plentiful will your people be saved from starvation during the famine."

Bread stamp

This is the kind of bread stamp that the chief baker would have used. His job was to grind and sieve flour, then knead it with water and yeast to make a dough. He shaped the dough into loaves, then stamped them and baked them in an oven.

JOSEPH PUT IN CHARGE

✤ Genesis 41-42 ✤

Signet ring
A signet ring was a symbol of office. Joseph was given the king's ring as a sign that the king had transferred his royal authority to him. The ring was used to stamp the king's personal seal on official documents. Joseph would have worn it on his finger, or on a cord around his neck.

Crops
Along the banks of the Nile, conditions were ideal for growing crops. The climate was sunny, and there were lots of workers. Every year, the Nile flooded and water spread on to the land around it. This made the soil rich and fertile. Farmers cut special canals and channels to spread the flood waters on to the fields.

Egyptian cat goddess
The Egyptians worshipped many gods. Some of them represented particular powers of nature, such as the sun, or the Nile floods. The cat goddess, Bastet, was the daughter of the sun god, Re. Bastet was believed to have the power of the sun to ripen crops.

Once Joseph had explained his dreams to him, the king realized what a wise man Joseph was. Clearly, he could hear God and was the right person to make sure that Egypt did not fall into ruin because of the coming famine.

"I now make you chief minister over all of Egypt!" the king declared, giving Joseph some smart clothes, a gold chain, and even putting one of his own royal signet rings on Joseph's finger to show his new authority. What a change – from prisoner to minister!

Now Joseph had to set about making sure there was enough food to feed the people. For the next seven years, there were plentiful harvests, just as God had said there would be. Joseph travelled around the country, collecting food from the fields and taking it to the cities to be stored. Corn was piled so high that it looked like millions of grains of sand on a beach, and Joseph gave up trying to measure how much there was.

Then, just as God had said, there were seven years of dreadful famine, when the crops in the fields did not grow. The Egyptian people were in danger of starving and they cried out to their king for food. The king told them to go to Joseph.

Now Joseph could put God's plan into action. He opened up the storehouses and sold the corn that he had carefully kept from the plentiful harvests. In fact, there was so much corn that many people from other countries came to Egypt to buy some for themselves because they were suffering from famine, too.

Joseph's family in Canaan also had no food, so Jacob told his sons, "Go to Egypt and buy some corn, so that we will not starve to death."

So Joseph's brothers travelled to Egypt. But remembering the tragic loss of his favourite son, Joseph, Jacob kept his youngest son, Benjamin, safely at home.

JOSEPH FEEDS HIS FAMILY

✤ **Genesis 42-45** ✤

Joseph's brothers did not recognize him as they bowed before the mighty Egyptian minister. Joseph pretended not to know them either. "You are spies," he accused them, harshly.

"No!" they protested. "We are an honest family. We have just come to buy food. There were twelve of us, but one of our brothers is dead, and our youngest brother is at home."

But Joseph had his brothers thrown into prison. After three days, he said to them, "If you want to save yourselves from death, bring your youngest brother to me. I will keep Simeon here as a hostage until you return to prove your honesty."

"Now we are paying the price for what we did to Joseph," Reuben sadly told his brothers. Joseph overheard this, and wept. He felt sorry for his family, so he let his brothers take home some corn.

Once they were back in Canaan, the family soon ate all the corn and Jacob reluctantly had to agree to let the brothers take Benjamin back to Egypt.

When Joseph saw Benjamin again, he was so pleased that he went outside and wept tears of joy. Then he treated his brothers to a magnificent feast.

Later, Joseph had their sacks filled with food. He also hid his special silver cup in Benjamin's sack, to test whether his brothers had become better people. When the missing cup was found in Benjamin's sack, the brothers were all arrested.

"You are guilty, so now you must become my slave," Joseph told the frightened Benjamin.

Judah was worried. "Our father has already lost Joseph. If he loses Benjamin too, he will die of grief. I will become your slave instead." All those years ago, Judah had been the one who suggested selling Joseph into slavery, yet now he wanted to sacrifice himself to free Benjamin.

Joseph cried with relief. "Don't you see? It is me, Joseph! God sent me to rule Egypt so I could save you from starving." He hugged his excited brothers. "Tell my father that you must all come and live here in Egypt, where there is plenty of food."

Egyptian silver cup
At the time of Joseph, silver was a precious metal that had to be imported into Egypt from Syria, so it was very valuable. Only noble men and women would have drunk from silver cups; ordinary people had cups made of pottery. The theft of Joseph's cup was a serious matter, not only because it was very valuable, but also because of Joseph's important position as chief minister.

POWER TO HELP OTHERS
In this story, Joseph is able to use his powerful position to help his brothers. You may sometimes be in a powerful position, too. For example, if a new boy or girl joins your class at school, they may feel lonely, or even a bit scared. If you have a big group of friends and know your way around the school, you are in a much more powerful position. It is good to use this power properly, by being kind to the new person and helping them to settle in.

A BABY IN THE REEDS

✤ Exodus 1-2 ✤

The king of Egypt was frightened by the many Israelites living in his country. He treated them very cruelly, making them slaves. Then the king told the midwives who helped the Hebrew women give birth to kill the babies if they were boys. But the midwives respected God so did not obey the king.

Finally, the king ordered, "Drown their baby boys in the river Nile!"

One Hebrew woman had a lovely son and didn't want him to be killed. She kept him at home until he was three months old and she could hide him no longer. She made a floating papyrus basket, placed him in it and gently pushed it off into the Nile.

"Watch what happens," the mother said to her daughter Miriam. As the boat bobbed in the reeds near the bank, the king's daughter and her servants came to swim. She noticed the basket, and as she peered inside the baby began to cry.

"It's a poor Hebrew baby," the princess exclaimed in amazement.

Seeing that she felt sorry for the baby, his sister bravely approached the princess and asked, "Shall I fetch a Hebrew lady to nurse the child?"

"Yes, go," she replied and so Miriam raced off to fetch her mother.

"Look after this child for me and I will pay you," the king's daughter told her. So the child's natural mother cared for him until he was older. The king's daughter adopted him and named him Moses.

Nile crocodile
Crocodiles are no longer found in the waters of the Nile below the Aswan Dam, but in the time of Moses they were numerous. Regarded as sacred by the Egyptians, crocodiles are the largest of all existing reptiles and can grow to well over 6 metres. Leaving a baby in a basket in the reeds of the Nile was very risky.

The finding of Moses
Moses was found in the papyrus reeds of the Nile by the king's daughter. She adopted him as her son, and gave him the name Moses, which sounds like the Hebrew for "drawn out of the water".

MOSES STANDS ON HOLY GROUND

✤ Exodus 3-4 ✤

When Moses grew up, he left Egypt and became a shepherd. One day he saw a bush on fire, but despite the flames the bush wasn't burning up at all.

He went over to get a closer look and the voice of God from inside the strange bush called to him, "Don't come any nearer! Take your sandals off because you are standing on holy ground. I am the God of Abraham, Isaac, and Jacob." Moses trembled with fear.

"I have seen the sorrow of my people in Egypt. I have heard their cries of suffering at the hands of their cruel masters and have decided to rescue them from Egypt and take them to a wonderful land full of everything that they will need. I have chosen you to go to the king and demand that he allows them to leave."

Moses thought up one excuse after another. Every time he thought of a reason for not going, God overruled it.

When Moses asked him how to reply if he was asked who had sent him, God told him to say, "Tell them 'I AM WHO I AM' has sent you." God also assured him that he would prove his power by performing great miracles.

Moses was still unsure. "I really don't want to do it. Please send somebody else!"

This time God became angry and thundered, "Very well then. I will send your brother Aaron to do the talking." So the two of them set out nervously for Egypt.

Shepherd and flock
Sheep were important animals because they provided people with milk, meat and wool for clothes. They were not kept in fields but roamed over the land, which was also home to wild animals. Shepherds protected their flocks and found them fresh water and grass.

Sandals
These sandals from the time of Moses are made from woven papyrus, palm leaves and grass. From their open design it is easy to understand how dusty the feet would get on a journey and to appreciate the need for the ritual foot washing. Removing one's sandals was a sign of respect in the presence of God, a custom still observed in Muslim, Hindu and Buddhist temples today.

Yahweh
These letters are Hebrew for "Yahweh" which translates as "I am who I am". There are several names for God in the Bible, but Yahweh is considered to be his most sacred name by the Jewish people and they do not pronounce it. In English bibles it is usually written as "The Lord".

PLAGUES STRIKE AT EGYPT

✤ **Exodus 5-10** ✤

Ramses II
Ramses II was also known as Ramses the Great because of the enormous temples and statues he built during his 67-year reign. Records show that much of this building work was done using slave labour. He was also a great military leader. The date of the Exodus is uncertain, so while some scholars believe that it happened during the reign of Ramses II, we cannot be certain.

Cobra
A cobra was one of the symbols of the Egyptian king's power and a representation of it was worn on the front of his royal head-dress, supposedly to spit fire at his enemies. The venom of the cobra works by paralyzing the nervous system. When Aaron turned his staff into a snake it was probably a cobra.

Aaron and Moses presented themselves to the king of Egypt. "The Lord God of Israel says you are to let his people go so that they may hold a festival in the desert to honour him."

But the king replied, "Who is this God? I certainly will not let the Israelites go."

So incensed was he by the request that he made the life of the slaves even more difficult. From now on they even had to make the bricks for the great temples they were being forced to build.

When Moses realized how distressed they were, he prayed again to God.

"Go back to the king. Even though he will do everything he can to resist me, he will eventually see my power and let you go," came the reply from God.

Once more Moses and Aaron appeared before the king of the Egyptians. While they were there, Aaron threw down his staff and it became a snake, but when the king saw his own magicians do the same thing he was unimpressed and stubbornly refused to listen to Moses.

God then told Moses to announce to the king that the river Nile would turn into blood. When it happened the king was still unmoved and so God brought a succession of dreadful plagues upon Egypt: he sent frogs that found their way into the people's houses; then irritating gnats appeared from nowhere; after they had gone flies swarmed throughout the land covering all the people and animals; then the animals of Egypt were struck down with a mysterious disease; next horrible boils broke out on all the Egyptians; hail destroyed crops and killed the livestock in the fields; then a dark cloud of locusts came down and stripped the countryside of vegetation; finally the whole land was shrouded in darkness for three days.

During each plague the king said that the people could leave, but when Moses stopped it, he changed his mind.

When Moses went to see the king after this final plague, the king said the people could go.

Moses told him, "We must also take our animals with us so that we can make sacrifices to God."

DEATH PASSES OVER GOD'S PEOPLE

✤ Exodus 11-12 ✤

Before his last meeting with the king, God had told Moses, "I will send one last plague upon Egypt, after which the king will expel you from his country."

At the end of his interview with the king, Moses told him what the final plague would be: "At midnight God will pass throughout your country and every first-born male from the highest to the lowest will be killed. The whole of Egypt will resound to the anguished tears of mourning parents. Only my people will be spared this tragedy. Then you will send your officials to me begging us to leave."

Moses then stormed out of the king's presence for the last time and went to his people to prepare them for the dramatic events of the night.

"Listen carefully to everything I have to say," he told the Israelites. "Each family is to choose a lamb and kill it this evening. Then they are to coat some blood on the doorposts. Then you must go inside and close the door tightly; no one is to venture out because God will pass through the land. Wherever he sees blood on the doorpost he will pass over that house. Every year you must do the same thing to remind you and your children of the way in which God killed the Egyptians, yet spared his own people the Israelites."

The people did as Moses told them and that night God kept his promise. Every Egyptian household lost a son, struck dead by God.

Early next morning the king sent messengers to Moses, pleading with him to leave. As the sun rose, the Israelites set off, driving their flocks past anguished groups of Egyptians who watched them walk off to freedom in the desert.

Hyssop
Although hyssop is mentioned many times in the Bible we are not certain of the plant's identity. Hyssop was used in the passover rites, for the purification of lepers, as a cure for plague, and in sacrifices. The herb we know as hyssop today grows throughout southern Europe.

PASSOVER FESTIVAL
The deliverance of the Israelites (the Jewish nation) from slavery in Egypt is commemorated by the Passover Festival. The word "passover" recalls how God allowed the plague to pass over the homes of the Israelites. Each year the festival is celebrated in Jewish households with a special meal of roasted lamb, unleavened bread and bitter herbs.

CROSSING THE RED SEA

✤ **Exodus 13-15** ✤

Chariot horse
Egyptian chariot horses drew two-wheeled vehicles which were used not only in warfare, but also for hunting, or as a means of transport for wealthy or noble people. The battle chariots of the Egyptian army which pursued the Israelites were designed to be stable, fast and easy to manoeuvre. They were fitted out to hold bows, arrows and spears and were used as firing platforms.

When he led the Israelites out of Egypt, God directed them towards the Red Sea along the desert route. During the day he gave them a bright pillar of cloud to follow and at night they were to follow a glowing pillar of fire.

When the king of Egypt was informed of the departure of the people, he regretted his decision to let them go.

"What have I done? We need those Israelites to work for us. Let's go and bring them back." So he assembled his army and, leading the way in his chariot, set off after the Israelites.

When the people saw dust in the distance they knew that the king had changed his mind. With the Egyptians behind them and the Red Sea in front of them they realized that they were trapped.

Terrified, they shouted at Moses, "Why have you brought us all this way to die in the desert? It would have been better to be slaves of the Egyptians rather than be slaughtered here in this dreadful place."

Moses replied, "Don't be afraid. God will rescue us today and kill every one of those Egyptians galloping towards us."

God then said to Moses, "Point your staff over the sea and I will push back the water so that my people can pass safely over on dry land." When Moses did as God commanded, the water divided in the middle leaving a dry path. Nervously at first, and then with increasing confidence, the Israelites scurried across to the other side between the two walls of water.

When the Egyptians attempted to cross too, God told Moses to raise his staff towards the sea again. As he did so the water crashed over the Egyptians, sweeping them away to their deaths.

The Israelites were so thankful for their remarkable deliverance that they joyfully celebrated their victory over the Egyptians with singing and dancing before continuing on their journey.

GOD FEEDS HIS PEOPLE

✤ Exodus 16-17 ✤

After a few weeks in the desert the Israelites began to grumble to Moses. "In Egypt we were never hungry, but since we have been following you we haven't had enough to eat. It would have been better to have died in Egypt!"

Moses replied, "This evening you will see how God looks after you even though you are complaining about him. When you eat meat tonight and fresh bread tomorrow morning, then you will realize that God cares for you."

Later that evening birds called quails appeared and the next morning the Israelites found food called manna lying on the ground.

"This is the special food that God is sending you," Moses told the people. "You are to collect as much as you need each day and once a week you must gather double so that you don't have to work on the Sabbath, which is to be a day free from work." For all the time that the Israelites were in the desert God provided manna and quails for them, and they were never hungry again.

The desert was hot and sticky and the Israelites needed water as well as food, but it was difficult to find. One day they camped where there was no water anywhere. Again they began to complain, "We're dying of thirst. We have come all this way only to die."

Moses asked God what he should do, for the people were ready to kill him. "Go to Horeb and strike the large rock there. When you do, enough water will come out for everyone to drink."

Moses followed God's command and enough water gushed from the rock for everyone to quench their thirst. So despite their moaning, God ensured that the Israelites had plenty to eat and drink during their travels.

SEND IN THE SPIES

✤ **Joshua 1-2** ✤

Flax plant
Flax is the oldest known textile fibre. It was used for making linen and rope. The plants were pulled up by the roots, soaked in water, and beaten to separate the fibres from the stalk. Women usually did this work. Then they would spread the fibres on the flat roofs of their homes to dry before spinning.

After Moses had died, God told Joshua that he would lead him and the people to victory. Knowing that Joshua faced many difficult situations, God spoke to him many times about the need to be brave and full of courage.

Before the Israelites entered the Promised Land, Joshua secretly called two men and told them to go and spy out the land, especially the city of Jericho.

The two spies did as they had been commanded. In Jericho, they stayed at the house of a woman called Rahab. But the king of Jericho heard that there were spies in the city. He sent his messengers to tell Rahab to hand over the men.

Rahab replied, "Two men did come to me, but they left late this afternoon and I do not know where they went." In fact she had hidden the spies under some bundles of flax on her roof.

When the messengers had gone, Rahab climbed up onto her roof to talk to the men. "The whole country is terrified of the Israelites," she said. "No one thinks that we can resist you, for your God is the only God in the whole world. Promise me that you will repay the kindness I have shown you – do not kill my family."

The men replied, "You have saved our lives, and we will save you. We will make sure that you and your family are not harmed when God gives us your land."

Rahab's house was built into the city wall and so she was able to let them down on a rope from her window. As they left, the men said, "You must gather all your relatives in your house. Then place a scarlet cord in the window, so that we know not to attack your house. Above all, do not tell anyone what we are about to do."

Rahab agreed, and the men went back to Joshua. He was delighted when he heard their news. "If the people are all afraid of us, then God will certainly give us the land," he exclaimed.

FLAT-ROOFED HOUSES
The traditional flat roof was constructed by laying branches or reeds across wooden rafters. This formed a secure base which would then be covered with a thick layer of mud plaster. The roof had to be replastered every year. In the summer, the family would often sleep on the roof, as it was the coolest place in the house. The roof was also used to dry flax or foods, such as figs and raisins, in the hot sun.

THE RIVER STOPS FLOWING

✣ Joshua 3-4 ✣

Joshua moved the people to the banks of the river Jordan. Before long the order rang out throughout the camp: "When you see the priests carrying the Ark of the Lord your God, everyone is to pack up and follow it. Prepare yourselves, because tomorrow God will perform a great miracle."

Then God said to Joshua, "Tell the priests to take the Ark to the edge of the water."

Joshua called out to the Israelites, "Listen to what God says. The Ark is going ahead of you into the river. As soon as the priests set foot in the water, the river will stop flowing."

Even though the river was in full flood, as soon as the soles of the priests' feet touched the water, it stopped flowing. The priests continued walking until they were in the middle of the river. Then they stopped, and all the people crossed over.

When the last of the people had reached the other bank, God spoke to Joshua again. "Pick a man from each tribe and tell them to find twelve stones from the middle of the river. They are to carry them to the other side and set them up as a memorial where you camp tonight."

When this had been carried out, Joshua ordered the priests to join the rest of the people. No sooner had their feet touched dry ground, than the river started to flow as it had done before.

Joshua then moved the whole Israelite camp to Gilgal. He ordered that the stones from the Jordan be placed there, and then he addressed the people. "When your children ask you the significance of these stones, you are to tell them that the Israelites crossed the river Jordan on dry ground. God did this, just as he dried up the water of the Red Sea for Moses all those years ago. He did it to show his great power and to remind you to honour him."

From that day on, the Israelite people respected Joshua, just as they had respected Moses, because they saw that God was with him.

Frogs
There are several species of frog in Israel. They live near water and in rivers like the Jordan. Frogs are only mentioned once in the Bible, in the story of the ten plagues of Egypt.

The river Jordan
The Jordan is the biggest river in Israel, and it is mentioned many times in the Bible. The Israelites approached the Jordan Valley from the east, and the river formed a natural boundary to the Promised Land. It was not an easy river to cross, as it could be forded only in certain places. Even these fords were useless when the river flooded its banks at harvest time.

Priest's breastplate
An Israelite priest wore a breast-plate, studded with twelve gemstones, one for each of the twelve tribes of Israel. It contained pockets for the Urim and Thummim, special stones used by the priests to cast lots.

STRONG ENOUGH TO KILL A LION

✤ **Judges** 13-14 ✤

Lion
In Samson's time, lions were common in Canaan. But their numbers declined and they eventually became extinct in the region in about AD1300. Lions normally lived in thickets along the river Jordan. But when the river flooded, they were forced out of their lairs and could be a real threat to people. Shepherds often had to kill lions to defend themselves and their flocks.

Honey bee
Honey bees were highly valued in Canaan. Honey was the main sweetener for food, and was considered one of life's necessities. A find of wild honey would have been a real treat. Wild bees often nested in clefts in rocks, but sometimes they would choose other odd places, like the carcass of the dead lion in this story.

After many childless years, God told Manoah and his wife that they were to have a son. "He must never cut his hair, for he is going to be a Nazirite, a man dedicated to God, and he will begin to free the Israelites from their enemies the Philistines." In due course, the child was born, and they called him Samson.

When he was older, Samson fell in love with a Philistine woman. He asked his parents to arrange a marriage. They were horrified. "What is wrong with one of our Israelite women?" they asked. "Why do you want to marry a foreigner?"

But he insisted, and so Samson and his parents went to visit the woman. As they approached the town where she lived, a lion attacked them. With the power of the Spirit of God, Samson ripped the lion to pieces with his bare hands and left its body lying on the path.

Later, Samson returned that way for the marriage ceremony. He was intrigued to discover that a swarm of bees had settled in the lion's dead body. They had made some honey, which he scooped out and ate.

At his wedding, Samson remembered this unusual incident. He set some of the guests this riddle: "Eats from the eater, from the strong something sweeter."

None of the guests could guess the answer, so they secretly went to Samson's wife and threatened her: "Find out the answer or we will kill you and your family."

She rushed to Samson, weeping sadly. "If you really love me, tell me the answer to your riddle."

Eventually he told her, and she immediately went to the guests with the answer. They, in turn, found Samson and told him, "It is honey from a lion."

Samson was furious that he had been caught out. In a wild fury, he stormed out of his own wedding celebrations. He left his wife and went back to live with his parents.

SAMSON FALLS IN LOVE

Judges 16

Once again Samson fell in love – this time with a woman called Delilah. The leaders of the Philistines came to her and offered to pay her to find the secret of Samson's strength.

So Delilah asked Samson, "Explain to me how you are so strong, and what someone must do to overpower you."

He replied, "If someone were to tie me up with fresh bow-strings then I would be as weak as the next man."

So Delilah tied him up with some fresh bow-strings and then cried out, "Samson, the Philistines are here!" Immediately, he sprang up and snapped the strings as if they were cotton.

"You have lied to me. Tell me the truth," complained Delilah.

She kept on asking him until, worn down by her nagging, Samson finally revealed the real secret. "If my hair is cut off then I will lose all my strength."

This time, Delilah realized that he had told her the truth and so she sent a message to the Philistines, "Come back tonight because he has told me everything."

That night, while Samson was asleep, the Philistines crept in and one of them cut off his hair. When Delilah woke him, he discovered that he was unable to resist the Philistines. They captured him, blinded him and threw him in prison. But slowly Samson's hair began to grow back.

Much later, the Philistine rulers were having a feast in their temple when they remembered him. "Let's bring Samson out to entertain us," they said. So Samson was led in, and stood between the pillars of the doorway.

He prayed to God, "Make me strong just one more time so that I can pay back the Philistines for having blinded me." Then he pushed against the pillars with all his might. They crashed down, bringing the roof down and killing everyone inside the temple, including Samson.

With this last dramatic act, Samson killed more of his enemies than he had done in all the rest of his life.

Nazirite
A Nazirite was someone who was dedicated to God for a special purpose. Sometimes this was for a specific period of time, but in Samson's case, it was for life. The name Nazirite comes from the Hebrew word meaning "separated" or "consecrated". Nazirites were forbidden to cut their hair or to drink alcohol. They also had to avoid all contact with dead bodies, so that they remained pure.

A CARING DAUGHTER

✤ Ruth 1-4 ✤

Ruth
The law in Israel stopped landowners harvesting to the very edges of their fields, so that foreigners, orphans, widows and poor people could gather, or glean, any leftover grain. In Israel, in the times of the Judges, there were many unscrupulous men who harvested everything in the fields, but there were still a few good men, like Boaz who offered Ruth work and protection.

Bethlehem
Bethlehem is built on one of the highest hills of the Judean plateau, about eight kilometres south-west of Jerusalem and eighty kilometres from Moab, where Ruth and Naomi lived. Little more than a village at this time, it was surrounded by fields of barley (a more drought-resistant crop than wheat), which gave way to the dry pasture of the Judean wilderness where nomad shepherds grazed their flocks.

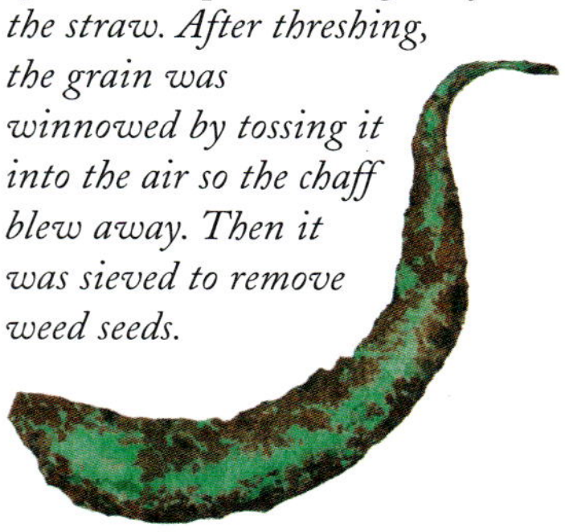

Bronze sickle
Men cut the crops with sickles, while the women bound it into bundles. These were threshed – beaten with sticks and trampled by oxen to separate the grain from the straw. After threshing, the grain was winnowed by tossing it into the air so the chaff blew away. Then it was sieved to remove weed seeds.

Naomi, an Israelite, lived in Moab with her husband Elimelech and their two sons. After Elimelech's death, the sons both married Moabite women. Tragically Naomi's sons died and she decided to return to Israel.

When Naomi said goodbye to her daughters-in-law, one of them, Ruth, said she would go with Naomi, saying, "I have decided to go with you. Your people and your God will be mine too and when I die I wish to be buried alongside you."

So together the two women went to Bethlehem and settled there.

At harvest time, Ruth went gleaning in the fields. One day Boaz, the landowner, asked his servants, "Who is that woman?"

"Ruth, who lives with Naomi."

Boaz approached her and said, "Ruth! Stay by my servants and glean all the grain you like."

"Why are you being so kind to me?" she asked.

"I've heard how good you are to my relative Naomi."

Ruth blushed and went on gleaning. That evening Naomi was delighted when Ruth told her about Boaz. She knew he would make Ruth a good husband. She told Ruth to put on her best clothes and go to see him one night after he had finished his meal.

As he was asleep, Ruth lay at his feet. When he awoke, he was amazed to see her.

"I would like you to marry me," he said, "but that right belongs to a closer relative of Naomi's. I will see if I can arrange to take his place as your husband."

Next day Boaz spoke to the other man in front of the town's leaders. According to custom the man had to buy a field that Elimelech had owned. When he did so, he would also have to marry Ruth. As the man did not want the field he let Boaz buy it – which also meant that Boaz could marry Ruth.

Naomi was thrilled. "Praise God," she said through her tears, "for through his kindness he will yet give me a grandchild."

HANNAH GIVES HER BABY TO GOD

1 Samuel 1-2

At that time in the hill country of Ephraim lived a man named Elkanah. Elkanah had two wives. Peninnah had children, but Hannah had none. Peninnah taunted Hannah, causing her great distress. It upset Elkanah too, because he loved Hannah. Each year they went to the temple at Shiloh to worship and make sacrifices to God. Peninnah would take advantage of the occasion to tease her rival even more. Elkanah tried to comfort Hannah, but she could not be consoled.

One year Hannah was overcome with sorrow and she prayed to God, "Dear Lord, if you look upon me with kindness and give me a son, then I will dedicate him to you for all his life."

As she prayed, her lips moved, although her words were silent. Eli, the priest, saw this and thought she was drunk. He rebuked her, saying, "Stop your drunkenness and throw away your drink."

Taken aback, Hannah replied, "I haven't been drinking. I am just a broken woman full of grief."

Eli apologized, "Then may God grant you whatever you have asked of him. Go in peace." So Hannah left the temple with her spirits raised.

In due course Hannah gave birth to a boy and called him Samuel, which means "heard by God".

When Elkanah made his annual pilgrimage to the temple, she stayed at home with the child, saying, "When he is weaned, I will take him to the temple to consecrate him to God."

When Samuel was older, Hannah did as she had said. She presented him to Eli at the temple doors, saying, "A few years ago you saw me praying silently to God. He has answered my prayer and so I have come here to fulfill my vow to him. I am giving my boy back to God in order that he might serve him all his life."

Eli was deeply moved by Hannah's faithfulness and praised God.

The high priest's clothes
A high priest, like Eli, wore special clothing to underline the importance of his role. All the clothes had a symbolic meaning. The beautiful breastpiece was studded with twelve gemstones, representing the twelve tribes of Israel, and also contained pockets for the Urim and Thummim. This was tied to a linen apron, or ephod, and worn over a blue robe fringed with gold bells and representations of pomegranates.

The menorah
The seven-branched lampstand, or menorah in Hebrew, stood in the Tabernacle. The menorah and all its accessories were made of pure gold, the cups shaped like almond blossoms. The menorah symbolized the glory of the Lord reflected in his people. Today it is the symbol of the Jewish state of Israel.

WE WANT A KING!

✤ 1 Samuel 8-10 ✤

Olive grove
An olive tree bears no fruit for the first fifteen years, but then it can produce fruit for hundreds of years. Olives were grown for their oil which was used in cooking and as a fuel for lamps, as a lotion for the skin and hair, and as a soothing ointment, as well as for anointing people to set them apart for God's service.

Cinnamon and Myrrh
The anointing oil was made from myrrh, cinnamon, cane and cassia. Myrrh yields a fragrant resin from its cut stems; cinnamon is obtained from the bark of the cinnamon tree; cane from the root of a reed plant; and cassia from the dried flowers of the cinnamon tree.

Anointing horn
Samuel anointed Saul to be the first king of Israel with sacred oil from an animal's horn like the one pictured here. As "the Lord's anointed", his leadership was to be spiritual as well as political. The horn of a ram, goat or wild ox could be used for religious or ceremonial purposes, but cows' horns were forbidden.

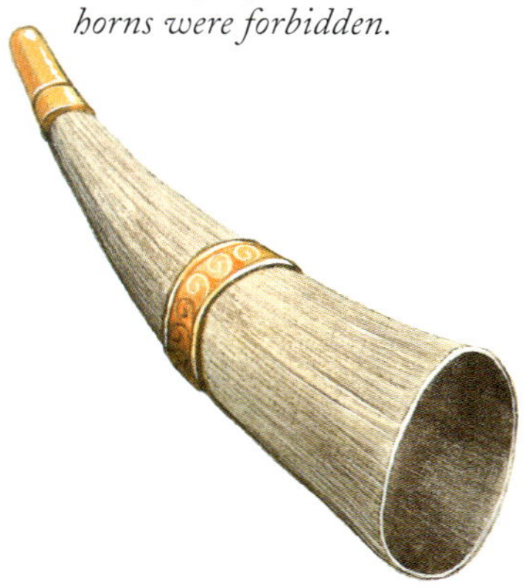

In his old age, Samuel appointed his sons to act as judges. But they were corrupt and used their position for their own purposes.

The leaders of the people met with Samuel and told him, "We don't want your sons, since they don't behave correctly as you do. We would prefer to have a king as the other nations do."

This request upset Samuel, but God said to him, "It is me that they have rejected, not you. Ever since they left Egypt they have been like this. You may choose a king for them, but warn them how he will mistreat them."

Samuel warned them of the consequences of having a king. "He will exploit you and order you to obey his every whim. He will take your land, your flocks, and your possessions. He will oppress you so that you will eventually call out to God for relief."

But the people could not be swayed.

"Very well," said Samuel. "Go to your homes and I will determine whom God has chosen to be your king."

Later, God told Samuel that he would soon meet the man who would become king. The next day Samuel met Saul, who was searching for some donkeys that his father had lost. Samuel invited him in for a meal.

Afterwards, as Saul was leaving, Samuel poured oil onto his head and said, "God has chosen you to be king. I have called all the people together and will reveal this choice to them. Make sure you are at the meeting."

When all the Israelites were ready, Samuel reminded them of what God had said earlier: "By choosing a king, you have rejected God's rule over you. But he has allowed you to go ahead with your plan. We will find the new king by drawing lots." They drew lots and Saul was chosen.

However, Saul was nowhere to be seen! He was so frightened that he had hidden himself among the tents and baggage that people had brought. So they brought him out in front of everyone.

"This is your king," Samuel proclaimed.

"Hurrah! Long live the king!" the people shouted at the top of their voices.

SAUL MAKES A MISTAKE

✣ 1 Samuel 13-14 ✣

Saul sent his son Jonathan to attack one of the Philistine outposts at Geba. He then sent messengers into all the land saying, "We have attacked the Philistines and now they are wanting to get revenge. All soldiers are to report to Gilgal at once."

Meanwhile, the Philistines prepared for battle. A vast army of them assembled, marched out and camped at Michmash. When the Israelite soldiers saw them they were terrified, and so they began to drift away back to their own homes. Those that stayed with Saul became increasingly scared. Samuel was due to come and offer a sacrifice to God before the battle. After a week he still had not arrived and so Saul decided to do it himself.

"What have you done?" Samuel asked Saul when he finally arrived.

"All my soldiers were leaving and you hadn't come. I thought I had better offer a sacrifice to God in order to seek his favour."

"You have done a foolish thing. You have disobeyed God. God will take the kingdom away from you and your children for ever. No one else in your family shall be king."

With that Samuel left Saul and his depleted army.

Meanwhile Jonathan went with his servant to ascertain the exact positions and strength of the enemy.

"With God on our side we can beat anyone, even though there are only two of us," Jonathan said to his servant. Stealthily they climbed up a hill and surprised a company of the enemy, killing about twenty of them. The Philistines panicked and ran for their lives. When Saul saw the confusion among them, he called all his men. They joined Jonathan and harassed the enemy all the way back to where they had come from.

Philistine head-dress
These Philistine warriors are shown wearing their characteristic battle head-dress of feathers rising vertically from a headband. The Philistines were warlike and a constant threat to the Israelites. Their military pressure was one of the reasons that Israel wanted a king. They had superior weapons made from iron.

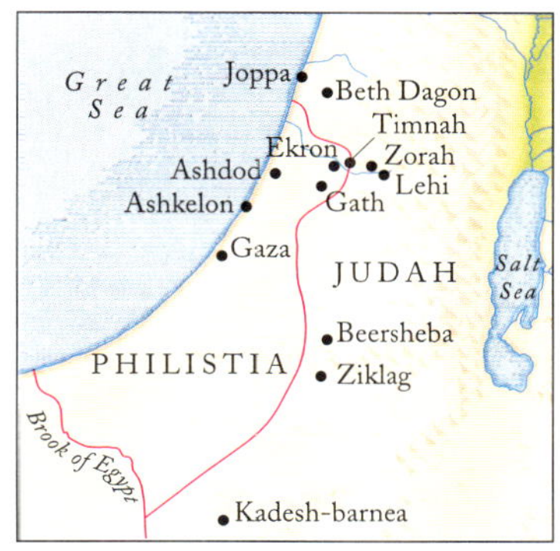

Philistia
The Philistines lived in five cities to the southwest of the land of Israel and bordering the Mediterranean: Ashdod, Ashkelon, Ekron, Gath, and Gaza. They gave their name to the whole of the land, "Palestine". They probably migrated here from the Aegean Sea.

Goat
In the Old Testament, a sacrifice could be made for various purposes: as a gesture of thanksgiving, or to make up for past sins. Only certain animals were suitable for sacrifice, including goats, bullocks, sheep, doves or pigeons. Animals for sacrifice had to be physically perfect, and male animals were preferred over females.

A SHEPHERD BOY IS CHOSEN AS KING

✣ 1 Samuel 15-16 ✣

Saul disobeyed God, who then regretted that he had allowed him to become king. Samuel too was very upset, but God came to him and said, "I have rejected Saul as king. Wipe the tears from your eyes and go to Bethlehem where Jesse lives. I am going to make one of his sons the next king."

When Samuel arrived in Bethlehem, he met Jesse and asked him to bring his sons to him so that he could meet them. As soon as he set eyes upon the eldest boy, Eliab, Samuel thought to himself, "This must be the one that God has chosen to be the next king."

But God said to Samuel, "Don't be swayed by his appearance, he is not the one that I have chosen. I look at things from a different perspective. People look on a person's outward appearance, but I look at what a person is like on the inside."

Next Jesse called Abinadab, and then Shammah, but Samuel knew that neither of them had been selected by God. One by one seven of Jesse's sons were introduced to Samuel, but none of them was the special one chosen by God.

"Do you have any other sons?" he asked Jesse.

"Yes, there is one more. But he is out looking after the sheep at the moment."

Samuel asked Jesse to fetch him. When David arrived, God said to Samuel, "He is the one. Anoint him with oil for I have chosen him to be the new king of Israel."

So Samuel poured oil over David and God's Spirit came upon him.

DAVID AND GOLIATH

1 Samuel 17

The armies of the Philistines and the Israelites faced each other across the valley of Elah. Goliath, the Philistines' champion soldier, challenged Saul's army. "Pick one man to come and fight a duel with me. If he should beat me, then we will become your slaves, but if I beat him then you will become ours."

His words struck fear into the whole Israelite camp – no one was brave enough to go out to fight him. Every morning and evening for forty days Goliath kept up his taunts.

One day, as Goliath was yelling out his threats, David arrived at the Israelite camp with some food for his brothers who were serving in the army. He was amazed that no one would fight Goliath. "What right has that Philistine to pour scorn upon the army of the living God?"

When Saul heard that David was in the camp he sent for him. "I will go and fight that Philistine, sir," he said.

Saul said he was too young, but David persuaded him with stories of his bravery when protecting his father's sheep from wild animals.

"Very well then, may God bless you," said Saul. "But use my armour." David tried it on, but it was too big. Instead, with just a staff, a sling and five stones from a nearby stream, he advanced towards Goliath.

When Goliath saw David, he let out a volley of curses. "Who do they think I am? Why have they sent me out a mere boy that I should slaughter him and feed him to the birds?"

David replied, "You can rely on your weapons, but I will kill you today in the name of the Lord God of Israel. It will be you who is eaten by wild animals, not me. Then everyone will know that this battle is under the control of God and that he is going to give us complete victory."

He then ran towards Goliath, put a stone in his sling, and threw it with all his might. It flew through the air, hitting Goliath in the middle of his forehead. Instantly the Philistine fell to the ground. David raced up to him, drew out Goliath's sword and cut his head off. When the Israelites saw what had happened, they rushed down the valley and pursued the disheartened Philistines and plundered their camp.

Goliath
The Philistines' champion was almost three metres tall and well armed, but David's victory over him proves that it is more important to have faith in God than to rely on size or strength.

Chain mail
The Bible tells us that Goliath's armour weighed about 56 kg and was made of small bronze plates punctured with tiny holes and laced together onto a cloth or leather tunic. The armour was completed with bronze greaves to cover the shins and a bronze helmet to protect the head.

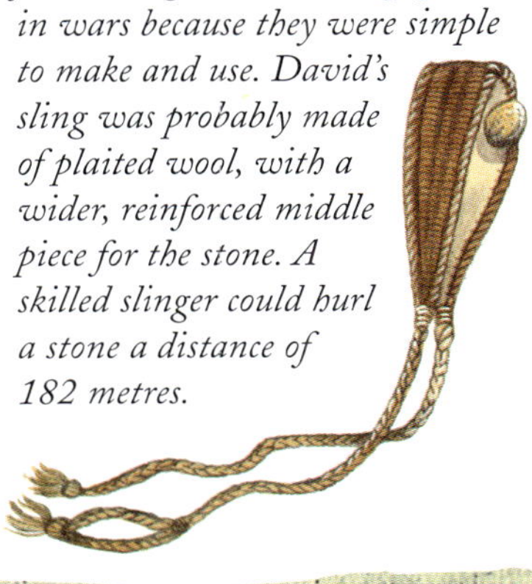

Sling
First used by shepherds to scare wild animals away from their flocks, slings soon became popular in wars because they were simple to make and use. David's sling was probably made of plaited wool, with a wider, reinforced middle piece for the stone. A skilled slinger could hurl a stone a distance of 182 metres.

SAUL ASKS A WITCH TO TELL THE FUTURE

✤ 1 Samuel 28-31 ✤

Inscribed bowl
Magic spells and incantations were sometimes written on bowls and other household utensils to ward off evil spirits. This Aramaic inscription calls on Gabriel, Michael and other good spirits to protect the house and bring healing.

Battle axe
The most common way of fighting a battle in Old Testament times was by hand-to-hand combat. Soldiers were armed with weapons like hammers, sticks, swords and axes. Although the sword is the most frequently mentioned weapon in the Bible, bronze axe heads of various shapes and sizes have also been found.

Isis
The goddess Isis was the patron of Egyptian magic. Using magic or sorcery to attempt to see into the future or to influence events or people was a common feature of the pagan cultures of the time, but it is always condemned in the Bible. God wants people to trust only him to meet all their needs.

Once again the Philistine army prepared to fight the Israelites. When Saul saw his old enemy paraded against him he was terrified.

Saul asked God to reveal to him what course of action he should take, but God would not speak to him.

In his desperation Saul said to his servants, "Find me a medium who will be able to tell me what I must do."

"There is such a woman in Endor," they told him. So Saul disguised himself and paid her a visit.

"I want you to call up the spirit of someone," Saul told her.

"But what about Saul?" she replied. "He has banished all mediums and spiritists. He would kill me if he found out."

Saul assured her that nothing would happen to her. "I promise you in God's name that you will not be harmed."

"Who do you want me to call up?" she asked nervously.

"Samuel," replied Saul.

Silently the woman began. When the spirit of Samuel appeared before her she screamed at the top of her voice, "Why have you deceived me? You are Saul!"

"Never mind that," said the king. "What can you see?"

"An old man in a robe."

"That's Samuel!" shouted Saul and he fell upon his knees.

"Why have you done this?" said Samuel sternly.

"The Philistines are about to attack us and so I asked God what we should do but he refuses to speak to me."

"If God will not talk to you why are you talking to me? You have disobeyed God and so what is happening now is merely the fulfilment of his word. David will become king after you. By this time tomorrow both you and your sons will be dead, just as I am."

Samuel disappeared and Saul collapsed on the ground in a heap. He was so frightened he couldn't get up. But the woman and his servants made him eat some meat and then he left.

The next day the Philistines attacked and there was a tremendous battle. One by one, Saul's soldiers were killed or deserted. Finally Saul himself died, just as the spirit of Samuel had predicted.

DAVID BECOMES KING OF ISRAEL

2 Samuel 2-5

Jerusalem today
The modern city of Jerusalem is much larger than it was in David's time when you could have walked around it in about half an hour. Today it covers an area of about 107 km² and has a population of more than 425,000 people, made up of Jews, Muslims and Christians. Most of the population live and work in the western side of the city.

After Saul's death, two people claimed the kingship. Some had chosen David while others wanted Ish-Bosheth, one of Saul's sons, to reign. Within a short period of time, the two groups were at war. It was a bitter struggle lasting a long time and many people on both sides were killed.

When Ish-Bosheth himself was treacherously murdered in his sleep, the Israelites knew that it was time for the bloodshed to end.

Representatives from all the tribes approached David at Hebron and said, "We are all part of the same nation. Let's put a stop to all this fighting. When you served Saul, God said that you would become our king. Now is the time. We want you to be king over us from now on."

David agreed to their request and so at the age of thirty they anointed him king.

Once David was established as king over all of Israel, he decided to make Jerusalem the new capital city. It was on top of a hill, and at that time was occupied by the Jebusites who had transformed it into an imposing fortress. David marched his army to the city walls.

The inhabitants were confident that their city could not be captured and so they taunted David and his men, "You'll never get inside! Even the blind and lame would have no trouble in keeping you out."

David issued a challenge to his soldiers: "The first soldier to kill a Jebusite will become the leader of the army."

Joab was the first to attack the city and so David gave him the reward he had promised, promoting him to commander-in-chief.

When he had captured the city, David enlarged it. He sent a message to his ally, the king of Tyre, asking for wood and stone to make a splendid palace. As he sat on his throne after many years of being an outlaw, he praised God for having made him king.

Carpenters at work
Hiram, the king of Tyre, sent skilled carpenters to help David construct the royal palace and build up the surrounding area. These drawings from Egyptian tombs illustrate the work carpenters did in splitting a beam, drilling, planing and polishing, sawing, and gluing wood together. Everything was done by hand.

Ruins of David's city
David made Jerusalem his royal city and the nation's capital. Its neutral location on the border between Judah and Benjamin enabled David to unite the kingdom. The city of David, or Zion, as it is also known, was about 12 acres in size, and had about 3,500 inhabitants. Built on the top of a hill with steep sides, the city was well fortified and almost impregnable.

WHO WILL BE THE NEXT KING?

✤ 1 Kings 1 ✤

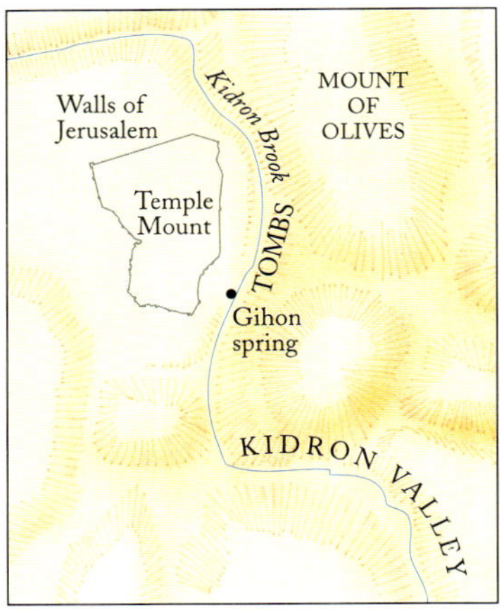

Jerusalem – the holy city
This map shows the layout of Jerusalem in the time of David and Solomon. On the west of the Kidron Valley was the Gihon spring. A channel through the rock took water from the spring into the city. David and his men used this route to capture Jerusalem from the Jebusites. To do so they climbed an 11-metre high vertical shaft and followed the narrow water channel under the city's walls.

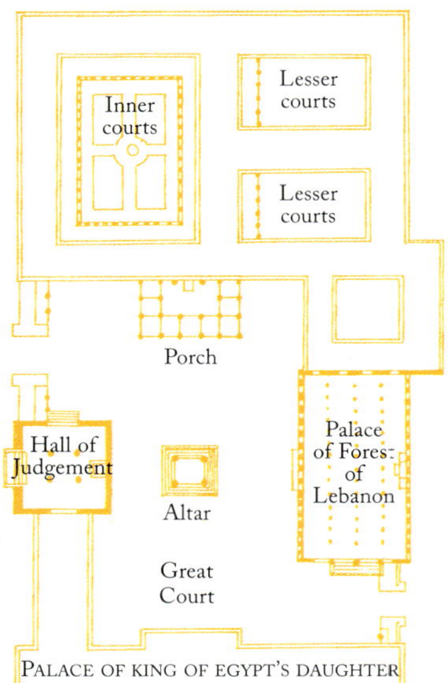

Solomon's palace
This is the floor plan of Solomon's palace, which he built when he finished the temple. The palace was magnificent. It was 45 metres long, 23 metres wide and 13 metres high, and took thirteen years to build. The walls were of stone and the roof was made of the finest cedar, specially brought from Lebanon, which is why it was called the Palace of the Forest of Lebanon.

David had now become very old and frail. Seeing how feeble his father was, his son Adonijah decided that he should become king. He made a series of sacrifices near En Rogel and invited his brothers and the royal court to the ceremony.

Then Nathan, who had not been invited, approached Bathsheba. "Have you heard that Adonijah has become king without David's knowledge or approval? You must go to David and alert him of this, reminding him that he has already chosen Solomon to take the throne."

So Bathsheba went in to see her husband and explained the matter to him. "Sir, surely you remember how you promised me that our son Solomon would be the next king? Instead, Adonijah has crowned himself king. The people are looking to you to see if you will approve this appointment."

As she was talking with David, Nathan entered and repeated exactly what Bathsheba had just said.

David then said to his wife, "I promise you by the living God that your son Solomon shall succeed to the throne after me."

Bathsheba was very relieved and bowed low before him.

David then sent Nathan and Zadok the priest to Gihon and told them to anoint Solomon as king.

When they arrived there, they did as the king had commanded.

At the end of the coronation a loud shout went up: "Long live King Solomon!"

Adonijah heard the noise and asked what was going on. When he was told that Solomon was the new king upon the express orders of David, he was alarmed. He fled and took refuge in the Tabernacle, because he was afraid that Solomon might wish to kill him.

When Solomon heard where Adonijah was, he sent some of his men to bring Adonijah into his presence and said, "As long as you do no evil then you will be safe, but if you sin then you will die. Now go to your home in peace."

CLEVER KING SOLOMON

✤ 1 Kings 3 ✤

One night God appeared to Solomon in a dream.

"I will give you whatever you request," he said.

Solomon replied, "I am still young and have no experience of how to rule. Therefore I ask that you will give me wisdom so that I might govern your people well."

His reply pleased God who then said, "Since you have not asked for wealth or victories for your own selfish ends, I will grant your wish. But in addition I will give you those things which you have not asked for – riches and glory, such that no other king alive will be like you. And if you obey me as your father did, I will give you a long life too."

Soon Solomon was given an opportunity to put his wisdom to the test. Two women came to him and one of them addressed him saying, "Sir, we live in the same house. We have both recently given birth to boys with only three days separating them. Last night she rolled over onto her boy and suffocated it. Then seeing that it was dead, she took my son while I slept and replaced him with her lifeless son. When I woke up I thought my child was dead, but after I had checked I realized that it wasn't my boy at all!"

The other woman interrupted, "That is not true! My boy is the living one. It is yours that is dead."

The other one answered back and soon they were arguing bitterly in front of Solomon.

"Silence!" he ordered. "Bring me a sword. Since you cannot decide between you whose child it is, I shall cut the living child into two and you can have half each." He motioned to his guard, "Cut the child!"

Then the boy's real mother fell on her knees, trembling and crying, "Please, sir, give her the child! Whatever you do, don't kill him!"

The other woman, however, remained cool and calmly said, "Neither of us shall have him. Cut the thing in two!"

When he saw the reactions of the women, Solomon announced his judgement: "Do not kill the child. Give him to the first woman. Only the real mother would behave in such a way."

When news of the king's verdict became public knowledge, the people of Israel marvelled because they realized that such wisdom could only come from God.

Solomon's horses
Solomon was a great horse trader and breeder, importing horses from Egypt and Asia and exporting them to neighbouring states. He kept 12,000 horses in vast stables in the cities of Hazor, Megiddo and Gezer. In fact horses became so common in Jerusalem that the city had a special horse gate.

BUILDING THE GREAT TEMPLE

✤ 1 Kings 5-8 ✤

Solomon sent messengers to Hiram, king of neighbouring Tyre. "God has granted me peace and it is my intention to build the temple that my father David proposed. I require wood from your fine cedar and pine trees for which I will pay handsomely."

So Hiram's men felled trees and floated the logs in the sea to where Solomon's men could collect them and take them to the site of the temple which took seven years to build. No expense was spared – either on the imposing exterior or the elaborate interior.

When it was ready, Solomon brought the Ark of the Covenant and placed it in the inner sanctuary of the temple, the Most Holy Place. When the priests who had been carrying the Ark left the Most Holy Place, the cloud of God's presence filled the whole temple.

Solomon and the people were full of awe and wonder. The king turned to everyone there and prayed, "Most majestic God, there is no god like you. You have indeed kept the promise you made to my father David when he spoke to you of his desire to build a temple. You have helped us from beginning to end and here today we thank you for your continuing love towards us. Yet even the greatest temple in the world could never be the home of the Lord God who made the heavens and the earth. Nevertheless, this place is yours: when anyone prays in this temple, listen to them and answer their prayer and forgive their sins."

Then Solomon blessed the people. "May the Lord bless you as he blessed our fathers. May he make you always love, obey and serve him."

For two weeks the people celebrated, offering sacrifices to God and dedicating the temple. When it was time to leave, everyone was full of joy at having seen the temple, and grateful for what God had done for his people.

THE QUEEN OF SHEBA

✤ 1 Kings 10 ✤

Before long, Solomon's fame and his faith in God became known all over the whole world. The queen of Sheba heard the impressive reports of him and decided to go to Jerusalem to see if the rumours were true. She arrived at the head of a splendid caravan, her camels laden with spices, gold and jewellery. She lost no time in conversing with Solomon, testing his knowledge on a wide range of matters. He answered all her queries with ease, explaining everything she wanted to know.

Solomon entertained her lavishly, showing her all over his royal city and outlining the laws by which he governed the country. He took her to the temple and explained the history of the Israelites and the miraculous ways in which God had intervened throughout their long history.

When the queen realized how wise Solomon was and saw his palaces, his court and had tasted the delights of his royal kitchens, she was deeply impressed.

Overcome, she confessed to him, "All the reports that I had heard about you are completely true. In fact, to be honest, what I heard touched only the surface of the truth. Everything here is far better than I could ever have imagined. Your people are very fortunate to have you for their king. The credit and honour surely must go to the Lord your God who has placed you in your exalted position."

The queen gave Solomon the gifts that she had brought and, in exchange, he gave her everything that she asked for, before she finally left, content and full of admiration, to return to her own kingdom.

Peacock
Solomon's trade expeditions probably reached India and brought back peacocks. In the early Christian church the eyes of the peacock's tail represented the all-seeing eyes of God.

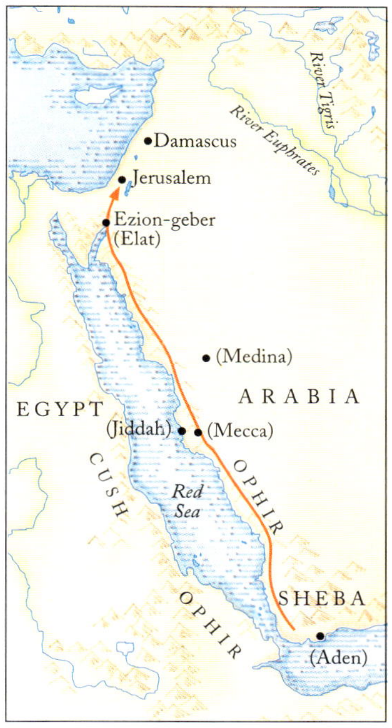

The Queen of Sheba's journey
The Queen of Sheba travelled from what is now Yemen in south-western Arabia, to Jerusalem, to see Solomon's wealth. Her journey was over 1600 kilometres and would have taken her through the Arabian desert and then along the main trade route from Arabia, the King's Highway.

Cedar of Lebanon
The cedar of Lebanon is a large coniferous tree. Its wood, valued for its strength and beauty, was always used for the temple's roof and wall panels.

TRAINED FOR THE KING'S SERVICE

✤ **Daniel 1** ✤

Fanning the fire
This wooden model from Egypt shows a man fanning a charcoal fire, which was probably used for cooking. Food was normally boiled in a pot over an open fire. To bake bread, large, flat stones were heated in the fire. When the dough was ready, the hot stones were taken out of the fire and the dough was placed on them to cook.

Spices
Like other ancient peoples, the Babylonians used spices to flavour their foods. One of the most commonly used spices was the herb cumin. It was grown for its aromatic seeds, which were ground up and used in place of pepper.

A diet of vegetables
The diet of vegetables that Daniel requested would have been fairly limited. Many vegetables, such as cucumbers, were eaten raw. Others, such as lentils, beans and leeks, were boiled in water or oil. Seasoning with garlic or cumin helped to give some flavour to what was otherwise a rather boring diet.

When the Babylonians captured Jerusalem, they selected a group of Israelites who had useful skills and took them back to Babylon. One of these men was called Daniel.

The Babylonian king, Nebuchadnezzar, ordered his chief official to select the very best of these young men. They were to be trained to help him rule his kingdom.

Daniel was willing to work hard for the king, but he also wanted to remain faithful to God.

When he realized that he would have to eat the same food and wine as the king, including foods forbidden by his faith, Daniel asked the chief official if he could eat a plainer diet.

"I am sorry, Daniel," the official said, sympathetically, "but the king has ordered you to eat his food. If you do not eat it and become weaker than the others, he will execute me!"

So instead, Daniel appealed to his guard. "Feed my three friends and me only vegetables and water for ten days. Then see whether we suffer or not."

The guard agreed. At the end of the ten days of their new diet, Daniel and his friends looked fitter and healthier than the Israelites who had eaten the royal food, so they were allowed to continue.

As Daniel followed his training, God gave him great knowledge and wisdom, and the gift of understanding dreams and visions. At the end of three years, the king questioned Daniel and found that he was much cleverer than his magicians. So Daniel became the king's servant.

Daniel explains the king's dream

✤ Daniel 2 ✤

King Nebuchadnezzar was tormented by a troubling nightmare that he could not understand, so he summoned all his wise men.

"You should be able to tell me exactly what was in my dream and what it means, without me giving you any details!" he insisted. "Unless you answer, I will have you all executed!"

"But only the gods can reveal such things," the wise men protested. At this, the furious king ordered that they should all be put to death, including Daniel and his friends.

Wisely, Daniel asked the king for more time. Then he went home and prayed that God would spare their lives by showing him what the dream meant. To Daniel's relief, God revealed the mystery to him in a vision.

"No man, including me, is clever enough to explain your dream," Daniel humbly told the king the next day, "but there is a God in heaven who can reveal all mysteries." Daniel explained that the dream foretold what would happen in the future.

"You saw an enormous and terrifying statue of a man," he told the king. "It had a gold head, a silver body, and bronze legs. As you were watching, a rock smashed the statue's feet which were made of iron mixed with clay.

"Then every part of the statue was smashed into tiny pieces that were blown away by the wind, leaving no trace. But the rock itself became a huge mountain which covered the whole world.

"Your Majesty, the gold represents your mighty kingdom, and the other parts of the statue represent other, less great kingdoms. And the rock that destroyed them all is God's eternal kingdom that, one day, will cover the whole world."

The king realized that Daniel was speaking the truth, and showed his appreciation by making him the ruler of the whole province of Babylon.

Babylonian boundary stone
The Babylonians kept records on clay tablets or stones. Sometimes records of who owned the land were made public and the stones would be set up in the field or temple to which the agreement related. Boundary stones like this one were marked with the symbols of the gods and goddesses who were believed to have witnessed the contract.

The Babylonian empire
The Babylonians reached the height of their power in about 600BC, during the reign of King Nebuchadnezzar. At this time, they controlled a huge empire, stretching from the Mediterranean Sea in the west to the Persian Gulf in the east. The story of Daniel takes place just after the Babylonians had conquered Jerusalem, in 586BC.

Signs of the Zodiac

Astrologers believe that the stars and planets exert a decisive influence on a person's character and destiny. Astrology flourished in Babylon under the influence of the priests. The zodiac and its twelve signs are thought to have originated there. The Bible rejects beliefs such as astrology, because God alone has control over the universe which he created.

THE FIERY FURNACE

✤ Daniel 3 ✤

The ruins of Babylon
Babylon was on the river Euphrates, about 80 km south of modern Baghdad in Iraq. It was the capital of the huge empire of Babylonia which it took over from Assyria. Under King Nebuchadnezzar the city was rebuilt and enjoyed fame and prosperity. Its "hanging" roof gardens were one of the seven wonders of the world.

Clay cylinder of King Nebuchadnezzar
This cylinder proclaims the rebuilding of the sun-god temple. Under King Nebuchadnezzar, many great structures were built. Their bricks were made from mud and clay mixed with straw. They were shaped into 30-cm squares, about 10 cm thick. Bricks were often inscribed with the name of the reigning king.

Musicians
These Assyrian-Babylonian musicians are playing (from left to right) the bagpipes, flute and harp. Musical instruments were made from many materials, including wood, leather, gut, ivory, shell, gold and silver. Music has been an important element of religious worship in every culture. Everyone had to bow down to Nebuchadnezzar's statue when the music began.

King Nebuchadnezzar decided to build a gigantic gold statue that all his subjects would worship. It was twenty-seven metres high and nearly three metres wide.

"As soon as you hear the music," the king's herald announced, "kneel down and worship it. Anyone who disobeys will be thrown into a fiery furnace."

When Nebuchadnezzar was told that Shadrach, Meshach and Abednego had refused, because as Jews they worshipped only God, he erupted with anger. "You have one last chance," he told them, "before I throw you into the furnace. What God of yours could save you then?"

The three stood bravely before the king. "Our God can save us from the flames," they replied, "but even if he doesn't, we still won't worship your gods."

The king's fury increased even further and he ordered the furnace to be made seven times hotter. So fierce were the flames that the soldiers who threw Shadrach, Meshach and Abednego into the furnace died immediately.

The king expected to see the three quickly burnt to a cinder, but his eyes widened with amazement. "Look! I can see not three, but four men walking in the fire. Come out, servants of the Most High God!"

Shadrach, Meshach and Abednego walked out. Their bodies and clothes had not been burned at all. They didn't even smell of smoke.

"Everyone should praise the God of Shadrach, Meshach and Abednego!" Nebuchadnezzar declared. "They were willing to die rather than worship any god except their own, but God sent an angel to save them."

The king was so impressed that he promoted them to higher jobs in his kingdom.

THE WRITING ON THE WALL

✤ Daniel 5 ✤

One evening, as King Belshazzar and a thousand of his most important officials were feasting, he issued a royal command. "Let us drink wine from the sacred gold and silver cups my father stole from the temple in Jerusalem!" he declared. After a while they all got drunk and started worshipping their idols.

Suddenly, in the light of the lamp, the king saw human fingers writing on the palace wall. His face turned white with fear, and his knees started shaking. The message was written in a language he couldn't understand, so he called his wise men together.

"Tell me what this means!" he demanded, but when none of them could explain, he grew even more afraid. The queen reassured him and told him that Daniel could help him solve the riddle.

"I have been told that God has given you wisdom to understand everything," the king told Daniel. "Now, if you can tell me what this writing means, I will make you powerful in my kingdom."

"I don't want any reward," Daniel replied modestly, as he simply wanted to serve God. "God says that because you have used sacred cups for your partying and have worshipped false gods, he has shortened your reign. He has weighed you on his scales and decided that you are not good enough to be king. So your kingdom is divided amongst the Medes and the Persians."

Despite the bad news, Belshazzar kept his promise and gave Daniel a purple robe and gold chain and made him a powerful governor.

That same night, God's message came true. An invading army killed King Belshazzar, and Darius took over his kingdom.

WORSHIPPING IDOLS

Idols are statues of animals and superhumans made from metal, wood or stone. God forbids the worship of idols. He wants us to worship only him. We can still worship idols today, because an idol is anything we put in the place of God, such as money, football, pop singers, even our friends. There is nothing wrong with any of these things, as long as they are not more important to us than loving God.

Daniel
God gave Daniel great wisdom, so that he could interpret the strange dreams of King Nebuchadnezzar. Now the new king Belshazzar needs him to explain the meaning of the writing that has appeared on the wall of his palace.

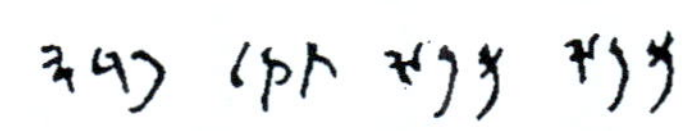

The writing on the wall
Archaeological excavations of the site of the Babylonian palace have revealed a throne room that was built in Nebuchadnezzar's reign. One wall is decorated with glazed blue bricks, while the others are of white plaster. On one of these walls Belshazzar saw human fingers writing the words MENE, MENE, TEKEL and PARSIN. The three words written in the Aramaic script of the 6th–5th centuries BC mean numbered, weighed, and divided.

Bull from the Ishtar Gate
Marduk, the chief deity of the Babylonians, was sometimes represented as a bull. Although we can't be sure what Nebuchadnezzar's 27-metre image of gold looked like, it was probably some kind of idol of Marduk. Marduk was honoured each spring at a festival where all the other gods came before him to supposedly determine the course of people's lives for the coming year.

DANIEL IN THE LIONS' DEN

✤ Daniel 6 ✤

Lion earrings
Lions symbolized power and authority. They were a popular motif in jewellery and art. An Asian species of lion once lived along the marshy riverbanks of the Tigris and Euphrates, and lion hunting was a favourite sport. In royal cities, lions were often kept in captivity, and could be used to execute prisoners.

Median nobles
Median influence was so strong in the Persian empire that Medes and Persians are often depicted side by side. This wall relief from Persepolis shows a noble couple dressed in typical Median clothes. The men's rounded hats and short tunics made them easy to distinguish from the Persians.

The Babylonian world
This picture shows the Babylonian view of how the world fitted together. At the top were the heavens, next came the air, whilst underneath and surrounding the earth were the oceans. Each of these three layers had its own gods: Anu was the god of the heavens, Enlil god of the air, and Ea "lord of the deep oceans". The king reigned as the representative of the gods on earth and was thought to be especially blessed by them.

Daniel governed so well that King Darius wanted to put him in charge of the whole of Babylon. But the other officials were jealous of Daniel's success. They searched for something wrong with Daniel's work so that they could get him into trouble.

But Daniel was so honest that they failed. So instead, they tricked the king into making a law. For thirty days, it said, people could pray only to the king. No one was allowed to pray to any other god, and anyone who disobeyed the law would be thrown to the lions as punishment.

Daniel knew that the new law was wrong and decided that he would carry on praying to God. At home, Daniel got down on his knees three times each day, as usual, and thanked God for his goodness.

But the wicked officials were spying on Daniel and one day they caught him praying and asking God for help. They rushed off to the king and told him, gleefully, "Daniel has disobeyed your new law by praying to his God. He must be punished."

Darius was horrified because Daniel was a wise ruler, but he could not change the law. So, reluctantly, he ordered his guards to throw Daniel into the den of snarling, hungry lions. Then the king lay awake all night, praying that somehow Daniel would escape.

The next morning, he ran to the den and shouted, "Daniel! Did your God save

you from the lions?" and waited anxiously for an answer.

Then he heard Daniel call out, "My God knew that I was innocent, and he sent an angel to stop the lions from eating me." Daniel's trust in God had saved him.

King Darius breathed a sigh of relief and commanded that Daniel should be set free. Then he ordered the wicked officials to be thrown to the lions instead.

COURAGE TO OBEY GOD
Daniel knew the king's law was wrong and he was prepared to disobey it, even if it cost him his life. Sticking to what you believe, even when this makes life difficult, shows that you are a courageous person. Sometimes this is hard, especially if it means going against what all your friends are doing. But obeying your conscience – the part of you that tells you right from wrong – helps you do the right thing.

Ruins of Babylon
The Persian king, Cyrus, captured Babylon without a battle. The Greek historians Herodotus and Xenophon record that the Persian invaders made their way into the city along the old dried-up bed of the river Euphrates. Then they launched a surprise attack while King Belshazzar and his nobles were feasting.

Darius the Mede
The Medes lived in the mountainous area of modern-day Azerbaijan and Kurdistan. In about 550BC they were defeated by Cyrus the Great and became allies of the Persians. When the Persians captured Babylon, they installed Darius the Mede as the city's ruler. Although the Bible calls him a king, he was actually appointed as a governor by King Cyrus.

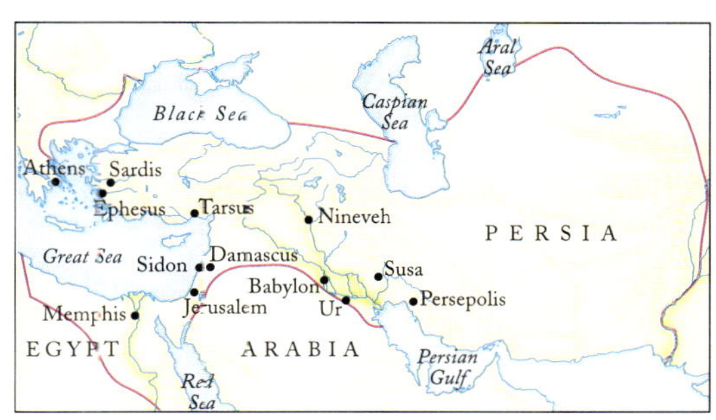

The Persian empire
The death of king Belshazzar in 539BC brought the Babylonian empire to an end, and marked the rise of the mighty Persian empire. The Persian kings extended their borders even further than the earlier empires had done. Persian control extended from Turkey and Egypt in the west, to India in the east.

A MIGHTY FISH SWALLOWS JONAH

✤ Jonah 1-2 ✤

Sperm whale
At about 18 metres in length, the sperm whale is one of the world's largest living creatures. Sperm whales are sometimes found in the waters of the eastern Mediterranean Sea, and their mouths are certainly wide enough to swallow a person whole. However, the enormous fish which swallowed Jonah need not necessarily have been a whale. Whatever it was, it certainly caused him to change his mind and go to Nineveh.

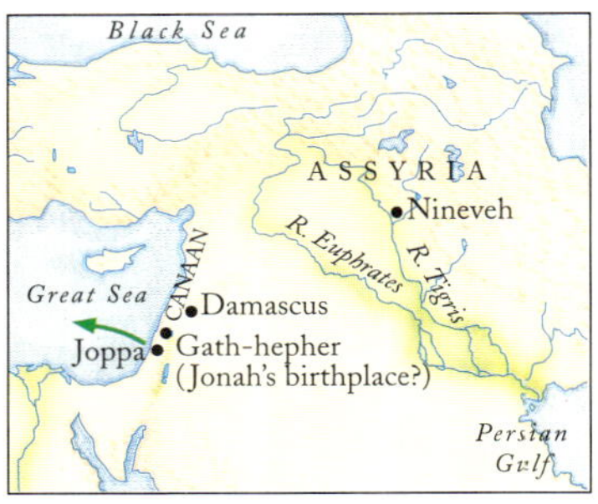

Jonah's journey
Jonah's mission took him on a journey of over 800 kilometres. God told him to go to Nineveh, but he boarded a ship for Tarshish - in exactly the opposite direction. Tarshish is thought to have been Tartessus, a port in south-west Spain. The fish left Jonah on a beach somewhere further up the coast of Canaan. From there he would have travelled overland to Nineveh.

Nineveh
The city of Nineveh is first mentioned in Genesis. It lay on the east bank of the Tigris river in modern-day Iraq. In Jonah's time, Nineveh was a royal city of the Assyrian kings. It later became the capital of their empire. Nineveh was surrounded by a brick wall over 11 kilometres long. It had fifteen gates, each guarded by enormous stone bulls. The wall in this photograph is a reconstruction of the city wall, made from old stone and bricks.

God told the prophet Jonah to go to Nineveh and warn the people about their wickedness. But Jonah was reluctant to go. He did not think that the people there deserved to be forgiven for their terrible crimes. Why shouldn't they suffer God's punishment?

So instead of obeying God, Jonah ran off to Joppa and got on a boat heading for Tarshish. But while Jonah was sleeping peacefully below deck, God made a strong wind blow and the boat was rocked by huge waves.

The captain of the boat was frightened and woke Jonah. "How can you sleep when we are in danger of being shipwrecked?" he asked. "You must pray to your God to save us all from drowning!"

As the storm continued to rage, the sailors cast lots to find out who was bringing this trouble on them. They discovered it was Jonah. "Yes, I must be the cause of the storm because I am running away from God," Jonah agreed. "The only way to stop it is to throw me overboard."

The sailors tried to control the ship with their oars, but the storm just got worse. So, reluctantly, they lowered Jonah over the side of the boat, knowing that he would probably drown.

Jonah sank under the crashing waves and got tangled in seaweed. Surely this was the end of his life, he thought miserably. But God had other plans. An enormous fish swam by, opened its mouth and swallowed Jonah alive.

For three days and nights Jonah stayed in the stomach of the fish, praising God for saving him. Then God told the fish to land Jonah safely onto the beach.

GOD FORGIVES NINEVEH

✤ Jonah 3-4 ✤

Once more, God told Jonah to go to Nineveh and tell the people to stop being wicked. This time, after his terrifying adventure at sea, Jonah was willing to obey.

Jonah walked through the streets, crying out, "People of Nineveh, in forty days' time, unless you turn to God, he will destroy your city!"

Everywhere he went, people took notice of Jonah's message and began to change their ways. The king of Nineveh ordered everyone to give up eating their fine food and to dress in sackcloth as a sign that they were truly sorry and wanted God's forgiveness.

God was glad that he did not have to punish Nineveh after all. But Jonah felt angry, and prayed, "Dear Lord, I knew from the beginning that you would be kind to these people, even though they are our enemies. I would rather have seen them all destroyed! I am so disappointed that I feel like dying."

Jonah went off and sat under a shelter he had made to watch the city, just in case God changed his mind about punishing the people. To protect Jonah from the fiercely hot sun, God made a leafy vine grow over the shelter to provide more shade.

But early the next morning, God sent a worm to chew through the vine so that it wilted and died. So Jonah was left miserable and uncomfortable in the scorching hot winds and sunshine, and he wished that he was dead.

"You should not be angry that I am kind to the people of Nineveh," God said to him. "You are unhappy about losing this vine. But you did not even plant it or care for it. Why shouldn't I be concerned for the many people who live in this city, and show that I love them?"

Castor oil plant
There is some dispute over exactly which type of plant provided shelter for Jonah. The Bible calls it a vine, but it could quite possibly have been a castor oil plant. This plant grows very quickly and has huge umbrella-like leaves which provide a lot of shade. The castor oil plant often grows in waste places near water, and is said to wither if it is handled even slightly.

RETURNING TO GOD

✤ Malachi 3-4 ✤

"How are we to return to God?" asked the people of Israel, who longed to receive God's blessings after so many generations in exile, but who didn't understand why life was still difficult.

"I have never changed," God explained. "I still offer you my forgiveness, if only you will stop stealing what belongs to me. Your whole nation is cursed by me because you don't fill the temple storehouse with the right offerings. If you give a tenth of your income back to me, then I will make sure that you have plenty of food. Watch me open heaven and pour out such a flood of blessing that you won't have room to store it!

"I will protect your crops from pests and make your grapevines heavy with fruit. Foreigners will see your rich harvests and say that you are greatly blessed by me.

"So stop saying, 'It's pointless to serve God and obey his laws. Evil people become rich so easily, and even those who proudly challenge God seem to get away without punishment.'

"Don't be mistaken. One day, my fierce judgement will burn them up like straw in a field, and they will be like mere ashes under the feet of my treasured children, those who love and respect me. Then my power will shine on you like the healing rays of the sun and your faithfulness will be well rewarded. Just remember to obey the laws that I gave to Moses."

The chosen people
The Israelites thought of themselves as God's 'chosen people' who were called to bear witness to his love and purposes for the world. Even though they often rebelled against him, he always preserved a remnant to continue his work. In the New Testament Peter says Christians are God's new chosen people, called to take the message of Jesus into the world.

MALACHI
Malachi was the last of the Old Testament prophets. The name Malachi means "my messenger". The prophet Malachi spoke of one coming who would prepare the way for the coming of the Lord. Such a one would come to purify and restore the true worship of God. The New Testament understands this reference to speak of the coming of John the Baptist, who made the way ready for the coming of the Messiah, believed by Christians to be Jesus.

Barley
Wheat and barley were the staple cereal crops in ancient Israel. Barley, pictured here, ripens before wheat and is harvested in early summer. It makes a flour and bread that is inferior to wheat, but because it was cheaper to produce, barley was often fed to animals and was the common food of the poor. Barley loaves came to symbolize poverty and worthlessness.